Animals That Travel

A sea turtle crawls back into the ocean after laying her eggs in the sand.

by Jennifer C. Urquhart

BOOKS FOR YOUNG EXPLORERS
NATIONAL GEOGRAPHIC SOCIETY

COPYRIGHT © 1982 NATIONAL GEOGRAPHIC SOCIETY   LIBRARY OF CONGRESS ⓒ︎P   DATA: P.32

In Africa, a huge elephant
squirts water into its mouth.
Another elephant reaches for
tree branches to eat. Because
they are so big, elephants
need a lot of food and water.
For part of the year, it is dry
where the elephants live.
Sometimes they eat
all the food in one place.
Then they must travel
to find more food and water.

WILDEBEESTS (*WILL-duh-beasts*) ON A MIGRATION (*my-GRAY-shun*)

Animals called wildebeests splash across a river in Africa.
The wildebeests are traveling to find grass to eat.
They move in a large group. Sometimes they walk in a long line.
Sometimes they crowd together. Their journey is often hard.

Many kinds of animals travel at certain times every year.
They travel to find food and also to mate and to have their young.
Some animals move on land. Some fly through the air.
Some swim through the water. Their travels are called migrations.

A bighorn sheep nibbles on plants in a valley. Other sheep cross a river in the valley. The sheep have come down from the high mountains for the winter. These mule deer are leaving the mountains. It is hard for them to find grass and other plants under the deep snow. The deer are going to a valley to find food. In spring, when the snow melts, all these animals will return to mountain meadows.

ROCKY MOUNTAIN BIGHORN SHEEP

Caribou live in Alaska and Canada. They are very much like reindeer. In spring, they migrate to places where there will be plenty of plants to eat all summer. During this time, the caribou also have their young. A caribou calf can run with the herd just a few hours after it is born. Caribou have antlers. They grow new ones every year.

BARREN GROUND CARIBOU (*CARE-uh-boo*)

ARCTIC TERN

WANDERING ALBATROSS

An albatross travels far
across the ocean to join its mate.
The albatross has long wings.
Each one is as long as your bed.
When they meet
on their nesting island,
the male and the female
do a mating dance.

10

Animals that fly can travel farther and faster than other animals. Arctic terns like this one are champion fliers. Some terns travel from one end of the earth to the other and back each year. This is probably the longest migration of any animal.

Snow geese take off after resting. Geese and other birds fly to warmer places where there is plenty of food in winter. A girl holds a whistling swan. Do you see the collar around its neck? The collar will help scientists pick out the swan on its migration.

Snow geese fly in a big V shape.
Birds called sandhill cranes
fly in the moonlight.
Other birds also migrate
at night. Scientists think
that they use the stars
as a guide. Birds that migrate
in the daytime may use the sun
to guide them. Scientists
are trying to learn more about
how birds find their way.

A Canada goose guards her goslings.
Their soft, fluffy feathers are called down.
One egg has not hatched yet.

In spring, many geese fly a long way
to find safe nesting places.
They usually return to the places
where they were hatched.
Goslings are ready to go into the water
soon after they hatch. They can swim
almost as well as their parents.
These goslings stay close to their mother.
She will protect them.

ALLEN'S HUMMINGBIRD

A hummingbird sips sweet juice from a flower.
The bird's body is smaller than your thumb.
Some hummingbirds migrate to warm places
where there are flowers and insects in winter.

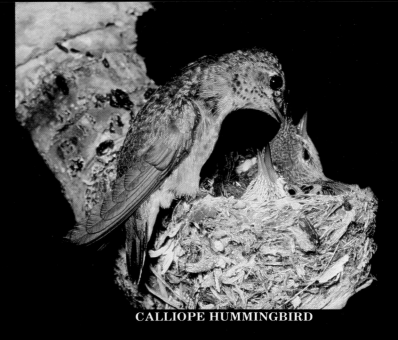

CALLIOPE HUMMINGBIRD

A hummingbird feeds her young.
Before they migrate, birds grow fat.
This gives them energy to fly far.
In their nest, baby house wrens
open their beaks wide for food.
Their mother will bring them insects.
In autumn, the wrens will fly south
for the winter. In spring, the parents
may return to the same nesting place.

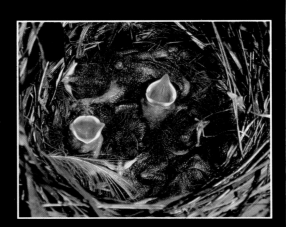

HOUSE WREN

Monarch butterflies rest on wild flowers in a field. They are delicate insects, but they migrate very long distances.

For a long time, no one knew
where monarchs spent the winter.
To find out, scientists in Canada
put tiny tags on their wings.
They asked anyone who found
a tagged monarch to send it back
to them. They learned that millions
of these butterflies migrate
to Mexico for the winter.
In spring, they fly north again.
Don't they look like orange leaves?

Ladybug, ladybug,
fly away home!
Some ladybugs,
or ladybird beetles,
also migrate.
In California, some
ladybugs fly
to the mountains
in early summer and
stay there until
spring. Then they
return to the valleys,
where the females
lay their eggs.

These locusts chew
on corn leaves.
Sometimes locusts
eat all the plants
in one place
and then fly to
another place.

LADYBIRD BEETLES

MIGRATORY LOCUSTS

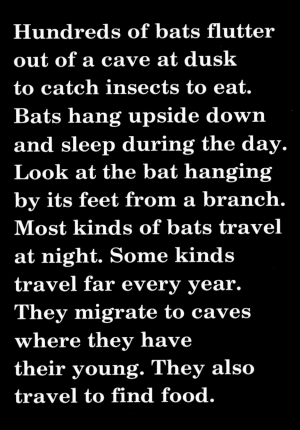

MEXICAN FREE-TAILED BAT

Hundreds of bats flutter
out of a cave at dusk
to catch insects to eat.
Bats hang upside down
and sleep during the day.
Look at the bat hanging
by its feet from a branch.
Most kinds of bats travel
at night. Some kinds
travel far every year.
They migrate to caves
where they have
their young. They also
travel to find food.

Splash! A humpback whale jumps out of the water. No one knows why whales do this. Maybe they are playing, or maybe they are signaling to other whales. Whales go on long migrations in the ocean.

Most of the larger whales live in cold waters. In summer,
they can find plenty of tiny sea animals to eat there.
In winter, they migrate to warmer parts of the ocean
to have their young. They eat very little then.
This mother humpback whale swims with her large calf.
They both have white markings on their flippers.

A harp seal rises from the water through a hole in the ice.
Most of the year, harp seals stay in the ocean.
In spring, they crawl onto the ice to have their young.
A mother harp seal lies with her pup on the ice.
How round she is! Her fat helps keep her warm.

Fur seals gather on a rocky island.
The male is much bigger
than the females. Do you see
the little black pups? When they
are bigger, they will swim far away.
In a few years, some of them will come
back here to have their own young.

NORTHERN FUR SEALS

A big red salmon leaps up a waterfall.
The salmon hatched in the river,
then lived in the ocean for a few years.
Now it is swimming back up the river.

A bear catches a salmon on its journey
up the river. Many of the salmon
reach the place where they hatched.
There the females lay their eggs.
In a few weeks, the eggs hatch.
A baby salmon gets food from the egg sac
on the underside of its body.
When the salmon grow bigger, they
will swim down the river to the ocean.
One day they will migrate up the river
to have their own young.

Penguins paddle through the ocean. They look as if they are wearing masks, don't they? Although penguins are birds, they cannot fly. They use their wings as flippers for swimming. Penguins live in the ocean most of the year. They migrate to the land to raise their young. After a chick hatches, its parents take turns guarding it and feeding it. When the baby penguin grows bigger, it will jump into the water and swim away.

MAGELLANIC PENGUINS

ADELIE PENGUINS

ROCKHOPPER PENGUINS

A big sea turtle pokes its head out of the water to breathe.
Sea turtles live in warm waters. When they become adults,
the turtles often return to the beach where they hatched.
The female turtles crawl out of the ocean and onto the beach.
Each one digs a hole in the sand and lays her eggs in it.
They look like little white balls, don't they?
After two months, a baby sea turtle hatches from its egg.
The baby turtle is about the same size as your hand.

The little turtles crawl as fast as they can to the ocean.
Would you like to follow the turtles and the other animals
you have seen and find out where they go on their travels?

Sandhill cranes fly
to their nesting
grounds. The cranes
call to each other
as they migrate.
This may help keep
the flock together.

COVER: A caribou
finds plenty to eat
at its summer feeding
ground in Canada.

Published by The National Geographic Society
Gilbert M. Grosvenor, *President;* Melvin M. Payne, *Chairman of the Board;*
Owen R. Anderson, *Executive Vice President;* Robert L. Breeden, *Vice President,*
Publications and Educational Media

Prepared by The Special Publications Division
Donald J. Crump, *Director*
Philip B. Silcott, *Associate Director*
William L. Allen, William R. Gray, *Assistant Directors*

Staff for this Book
Margery G. Dunn, *Managing Editor*
Veronica J. Morrison, *Picture Editor*
Cynthia B. Scudder, *Art Director*
Gail N. Hawkins, *Researcher*
Carol A. Rocheleau, *Illustrations Secretary*

Engraving, Printing, and Product Manufacture
Robert W. Messer, *Manager*
George V. White, *Production Manager*
David V. Showers, *Production Project Manager*
Mark R. Dunlevy, Richard A. McClure, Raja D. Murshed, Gregory Storer, *Assistant Production Managers*
Katherine H. Donohue, *Senior Production Assistant;* Katherine R. Leitch, *Production Staff Assistant*

Nancy F. Berry, Pamela A. Black, Nettie Burke, Claire M. Doig, Rosamund Garner, Victoria D. Garrett, Sheryl A. Hoey,
    Virginia A. McCoy, Cleo Petroff, Victoria I. Piscopo, Tammy Presley, Katheryn M. Slocum, Jenny Takacs, *Staff Assistants*

Consultants
Lila Bishop, Dr. Glenn O. Blough, Judith Hobart, *Educational Consultants*
Lynda Ehrlich, *Reading Consultant*
Dr. Archie Carr, Graduate Research Professor, Department of Zoology, University of Florida; Dr. Albert W. Erickson,
    Professor of Wildlife Science, University of Washington; Dr. Eugene S. Morton, Department of Zoological Research,
    National Zoological Park; Dr. George E. Watson, Curator of Birds, Smithsonian Institution; Dr. Timothy C. Williams and
    Janet M. Williams, Department of Biology, Swarthmore College, *Scientific Consultants*

Illustrations Credits
Stephen J. Krasemann, DRK PHOTO (cover, 25 lower); Mark Boulton, NATIONAL AUDUBON SOCIETY COLLECTION/PHOTO RESEARCHERS, INC. (1); National
Geographic Photographer Emory Kristof (2); Wolfgang Bayer (2-3 upper); Carol Hughes, BRUCE COLEMAN INC. (2-3 lower); National Geographic Photographer Bruce Dale
(4-5 upper); Joan Root, SURVIVAL ANGLIA LIMITED (4-5 lower); Peter Davey, BRUCE COLEMAN INC. (5); Sid Roberts, ARDEA LONDON (6 upper); James K. Morgan,
NASC/PR (6 lower); GRANT HEILMAN PHOTOGRAPHY (7); Stephen J. Krasemann, NHPA (8); Steven C. Wilson, ENTHEOS (8-9, 13 left, 32); Stephen J. Krasemann,
PETER ARNOLD, INC. (9); David and Katie Urry, ARDEA LONDON (10-11); M. P. Kahl (10); Francois Gohier, ARDEA LONDON (11); National Geographic Photographer
Bianca Lavies (12, 19 upper); Jeff Foott, BRUCE COLEMAN INC. (12-13); Richard Kolar, ANIMALS ANIMALS (13 right); Breck P. Kent, ANIMALS ANIMALS (14-15);
Laura Riley, BRUCE COLEMAN INC. (15); Bob and Clara Calhoun, BRUCE COLEMAN INC. (16-17); M. A. Chappell, ANIMALS ANIMALS (17 upper); William D. Griffin,
ANIMALS ANIMALS (17 lower left); George Harrison, GRANT HEILMAN PHOTOGRAPHY (17 lower right); Jim Brandenburg (18-19); Jeff Foott, BRUCE COLEMAN
INC. (19 lower, 27 lower); Mickey Pfleger (20 upper); Russ Kinne, NASC/PR (20-21); Jane Burton, BRUCE COLEMAN INC. (20 lower); Larry R. Ditto, BRUCE COLEMAN
INC. (21 upper); Robert W. Mitchell, ANIMALS ANIMALS (21 lower); Flip Nicklin (22); Sylvia A. Earle (22-23); Fred Bruemmer (24-25, 25 upper); Jeff Foott (26-27); Jeff
Foott, SURVIVAL ANGLIA LIMITED (26 lower); Will Troyer, ALASKAPHOTO (27 upper); Roger Tory Peterson, NASC/PR (28-29); Bruno J. Zehnder, PETER ARNOLD,
INC. (29 upper); Cindy Buxton and Annie Price, SURVIVAL ANGLIA LIMITED (29 lower); Runk/Schoenberger, GRANT HEILMAN PHOTOGRAPHY (30 upper left); C.
Allan Morgan (30 upper right, 31); Robert E. Schroeder (30-31).

Library of Congress ⓒⓅ Data
Urquhart, Jennifer C.
  Animals that travel.

  (Books for young explorers)
  Summary: Text and illustrations describe animals that migrate in search of food and favorable conditions for survival.
  1. Animal migration—Juvenile literature. [1. Animals—Migration] I. Title. II. Series.
QL754.U76   591.52'5   82-47856
ISBN 0-87044-450-6 (library binding)   AACR2